AF413149

AN EYE OPENER

Dedication

To my adorable father who taught me to look at life with compassion and sense of humour.

CONTENTS

FOREWORD

We live in a highly competitive world. The responsibilities and demands are galore. Sometimes we are so caught up with this hectic nature of life that we do not see the obvious happening right in front of our eyes. Or to put it straight, we just don't care. But there are people who are really very sensitive to even the little things that happen in their life or in the lives of people surrounding them.

One such is the author of this book "An Eye-opener *(anecdotes from real life experiences)*." This collection of articles expresses the author's understanding of the world around her. It is a reflection of her sensitive nature, the lessons learnt in life, her experiences and how she takes steps to transform the lives of the underprivileged. The themes of the articles vary. Engagements with the Visually Challenged people and how she tries to make their lives better, her professional life; she being a teacher, her classroom activities are discussed, life in general and the expectations from it, human compassion, lack of freedom and education is seen through her eyes. These are real situations of life and not imagined ones and therefore, we are tickled into thinking if we do actively participate in them, can we not really make a difference at all!

The fifteen articles are those nuances of life which otherwise goes unnoticed by people who are in the rat race.

They are a great read; they awaken the minds of the readers to the subtlety of life and also encourage people to think 'out of the box.'

Dr. INDHU M. EAPEN

AUTHOR'S NOTE

The sparkle in their eyes…the smile on their face and the mesmerized attention of my students as I narrate my experiences of life, urge me to live life to the fullest trying to make it more meaningful with my little contribution to this world of writing and publishing. This compilation of published and unpublished articles is my urge to set a precept…worthy of emolution.

I thank my students who have made me feel proud to present this documentation of my life's experiences which had been a part of their LSRW skills.

My special thanks to my dear friend Indhu Eapen who is always by my side correcting, guiding and enhancing my literary world.

I owe my gratitude to Dr. Mekhala Venkatesh for reviewing the book and boosting my confidence to go ahead.

I am also grateful to Notion Press team for bringing out this book beautifully with apt cover design.

I express my heartfelt gratitude to my parents and my brothers, who are responsible for nurturing me to be a person with finer sensibilities.

I run short of words to express my finest thanks to my dear family – my husband and my two darling children Shreyanka and Nishanth who have constantly encouraged me to go ahead with all my endeavours.

REVIEW...

When I befriended Prof. Prasanna Udipikar who at a college Board of Studies meet, my initial thoughts about her was that she's so composed and graceful. Later her enthusiasm to hold literary seminars baffled me and more surprise was in store when she requested me to do the honour of writing my response to her articles written over a period of time. That she found time to pen her thoughts into words while juggling work-life balance was commendable. While reading her short vignettes of life what I found truly admirable was that she didn't merely write about life's fellow travellers but also 'walked her talk' by working towards their betterment as in the case of her setting up a committtee to aid visually challenged students take up higher education. Her stories can be anyone's experience as she makes the reader empathise with 'Sakkamma,' ponder over 'Chimera,' laugh at 'Incorrigible Mosquitoes;' undoubtedly her students provide ample insights as she shares their experiences in 'Fun Grammar Class,' 'All About Love,' 'An Eye-opener.' I wish her success in all her future endeavours, which comes from my inherent belief that her 'middles' will soon put her on 'centre stage.'

Dr. MEKHALA VENKATESH

Department of English,

Jain University, Bangalore.

AN EYE-OPENER

Lecturing on Dr. David Herbert – the first visually challenged doctor, I concluded that considering physical disability as a hurdle to achieve one's goal is a myth. Determination complimented by unlimited effort and undeterred passion are the necessary ingredients to make life sweet and meaningful. Dr. Herbert, though blind, had a passion to study medicine and the goal to become a doctor. His aim in life was to rehabilitate people with psychiatric problems. Perseverance is needed to steer life to reach the set goal. Vision in life is more important than the sight. "I can...I will...I must" should be your words..."Dream big..."

Listening attentively in the class of eighty was Shilpa – a visually challenged student. I could see a confident smile on her face. I was sure my words had ignited a new hope in her...her confidence was kindled...'nothing is impossible' she had felt. Her aim in life was to pursue her studies in Commerce and Computer Science and join the corporate world by picking up a job in any of the leading multinational company. She had big dreams of pacing up with the current trend.

Shilpa scored First class in II PUC and joined Commerce stream for degree with a spirit to excel academically along with a dream of getting selected in one of the campus interviews conducted by the MNCs. But the path was not smooth...hurdles were too many...new atmosphere, new friends, new method of teaching, semester system, illiterate parents, poverty...the list of problems was perennial...she was lost in the maze of problems...she was all at sea!!!

A haggard Shilpa approached me one day and said "Madam there is no God...I want to give up" she cried relentlessly...rather vehemently. I tried to console her by recalling incidents from the life of Dr. Herbert and advised not to deter from pursuing her aim. Dismissing my words she said that Dr. Herbert's parents were rich, educated and his teachers helped him...Ah! she had challenged the teacher in me...how blindfolded I was!! Shilpa was blind by birth....Had I adopted blindness to the problems of my students? Visually impaired Shilpa was an eye-opener to her teacher...Like Chenna who had unveiled the problems of life to Siddhartha, Shilpa had enlightened her teacher about the problems of students like her...she had alerted the teacher's role and responsibility in the success of a student. I held her hand and assured her that she too has a teacher who has lots of concern for her. Feeling guilty I walked home with a heavy heart, thinking of the different ways that I could assist Shilpa...

Lines from Robert Frost's poem echoed in my ears:

The woods are lovely, dark and deep,

But I have promises to keep,

And miles to go before I sleep

And miles to go before I sleep

My guilt was so forceful that I ventured into recording my voice and preparing cassettes for all the necessary subjects. My gift of the cassettes bloomed a smile on her face and her keenness in listening to the cassettes left me flabbergasted. After her exams she called me and said in a confident voice, "Ma'm there is God!"

FUN GRAMMAR CLASS

The students were getting steered for Fun grammar class – a session where every student is made to participate, contribute and respond. As a tutor, these classes helped me in breaking the barriers that existed between the teacher and the students through mind-bogging exercises which brought the teacher and the taught closer. Intending to enrich the vocabulary of the students, that day I started off with a new game in the Fun Grammar class. I asked the students to write any four new words referring the dictionary or thesaurus and express their view of life in one short sentence. For example words like

'Exultant,' 'Jubilant,' 'Elated,' 'Ecstatic' conclude that 'Life is JOYFUL.'

I had suggested the students to think and choose the new words which must help them to express their perspective of life. The words could be either a group of adjectives or suggestive words which would help them to express the poignancy of their life's viewpoint. They were expected to write in a piece of paper and hand it over to me within 10 minutes as we were venturing into other vistas of grammar.

After the class, sitting alone I was amused at the young India's opinion of life. No doubt, the students were connoisseurs. They were pretty nifty in choosing the words as they had to express their outlook of Life. Browsing through the slips of papers was a humongous task, yet very entertaining.

Some of the samples worth to share are:

'Alluring,' 'Ravishing,' 'Enchanting,' 'Sensuous'

➤ Life is ROMANCE.

'Euphoric,' 'Rapturous,' 'Exultant,' 'Buoyant'

➤ Life is ECSTATIC.

'Dormant,' 'Comatose,' 'Quiet scent,' 'Torpid'

➤ Life is BOREDOM.

'Clandestine,' 'Covert,' 'Surreptitious,' 'Conspiratorial'

➤ Life is MYSTERIOUS.

'Exciting,' 'Thrilling' 'Sensuous' 'Sensational'

➤ Life is QUIXOTIC.

But the slip which churned my bowels and brought a twirl in my stomach was the one which carried the following words and the perspective of Life…

'Downcast,' 'Despondency,' 'Depression,' 'Dejection'

➤ Life is A PAIN.

These words and the student's attitude to life kindled my inquisitiveness which prompted me to talk to the girl. The cute, short girl followed me after the class with an anxious look. Deep into her big blue eyes I saw the articulation of PAIN. An affectionate smile and a pat on her back made the student comfortably sit beside me to unravel her story.

The PAIN was due to CANCER which had shattered and battered her for eight years. The girl who had fallen in love with the Fun grammar classes said, "Madam Cancer has – 'Nullified,' 'Traumatized,' 'Devastated,' 'Horrified' my life – hence

➢ Life is AGONY."

The doctor had advised her to get rid of her left leg for the relief from the PAIN. To lose pain and to gain relief…the bargain was colossal. Well versed in Hindi language, the girl said with a meek smile,

"Kuch Pane Ke liye Kuch Khona Padega."

Ah!.. . I was thunderstruck…tears rolled down blurring my vision as my dear student walked away…

After the vacation of two months, my dear student came to the Fun grammar class hopping with the crutches and gave me a piece of paper with a note:

'Crippled,' 'Incapacitated,' 'Disabled,' 'Maimed'

➢ Life is A CHALLENGE.

ALL ABOUT LOVE

That was a damp drizzling day and to my surprise the postman fetched an inland letter addressed to me. Pondering how even in these days of technology, somebody has resorted to the old system, I opened the letter. It was from an alumna of my college. The content of the letter is worth sharing as the traits of "love" were discussed and reattributed by redefining its grammatical role. Withhold the impish smile on your orifice as you move on to read…

My dear English teacher,

As a young girl when I bent and picked up the half eaten chocolate fallen on the ground to put it into my mouth, the maid hit my hand hard, snatched away my favourite auburn chocolate and threw it. I yelled at the top of my voice and created a ruckus, knowing little that it was an act of "Love" towards me.

When my father stared at me irately at the dining table instructing my mother not to permit me to get up from my place until I emptied the food served and gulped the milk… Little I understood the concern of my father about my health. With my eyes full of tears…trying to suppress tears rolling down my cheeks I thought that everybody at home including father detested me.

Every day, when my brother promptly and punctually came after my college hours to pick me up, little I understood his protective, shielding temperament towards his beautiful sister but thought that he was trying to curtail my freedom by being too bossy!!!

If today I have grown into a confident, efficient, multi-tasking person, it is because of the love constraints and not careless freedom.

When my mother forced me to keep my books, bags and other belongings in order, not to slouch but to sit and walk straight, never to waste time doing nothing but to induce life in my time…I wondered how mother could be so callous and vengeful towards her only girl child. My mind added fuel to the fire by contributing a thought that male child is pampered and not female child. I found all the disciplinary rules were annoying, making life irritating. Hardly had I known that these disciplinary exercises go a long way in making me a lovable wonderful person. Love does not only come in soft spoken packages but also in hard nutshells!!!

Now I have grown big and am married. I feel my husband in his busy schedule; hectic, affianced, engaged, unavailable, occupied hardly loves me. With all the credentials and reputation to his credit, I feel that he is good to others than to his wife. He loves everyone except me! He is too busy, yet he makes time to take me to hotels and movies, brings me things I like…but he is too harsh in his ways and I feel he doesn't have love for me. With a hope of putting an end to this hypocrisy and shun myself free from the shackles of marriage…

Commit to your memory…Walking down the memory lane you will be able to recall…twenty years back on a rainy day, storm in my heart I had approached you…when with your thick glasses you were immersed in correction of test papers, I had rendered my heart – my thoughts for your amendment. My favorite English teacher, you were the one who had taught that Love is an Abstract Noun in grammar class. Quoting Shakespeare you explained that Love is an eternal guiding force and a protective shield in life "Love is a Pole star to the wandering barks, though its height is known its altitude is not known…Love is not Time's Fool." Was love fooling me around? was my question to you. After patiently listening to my woes and hydra-headed self created problems, removing your spectacles and putting it aside, patiently…as patiently as Lord Krishna filled strength in Arjuna when Arjuna had given up the fight, you took my hand in yours and explained how "Love should be seen in the actions and not in mere words. Sweet nothings alone are not Love. To see love and experience it, there should be love within. Love begets love." Your answers to my questions were very satisfying. Apt examples from life, literature, media and movies enriched my heart and head both. Mind is an evil's workshop producing devil's broods. Devilish thoughts beget iniquitous results. The connectivity between the heart and head was established by our discussion. Argumentative, dismissive psyche turned into calm and caring mind. The layer of cataract which had blurred my thoughts and understanding was cleared. With all the Love in my court, I lived like a rhino which runs in search of the scent which is emitted from its own horns! You had cleared the air! I am now out of the wood.

Leading an affluent happy life, I salute thee teacher for helping me to save the beauty of love.

Love is an Abstract Noun in Parts of Speech but in real life it is a Verb. Love expressed through Concrete action helps in experiencing the Abstract form of Love!

Your Love filled student…

WOES OF THE SIGHTLESS STUDENTS

Case 1: Visually Challenged student appearing for II PUC exam is waiting for the scribe. At 9 o'clock the scribe calls up and says that due to some relative's death she will not be able to come to write the exam for him. Panicked student approaches the authorities who sympathize the visually challenged student and throw off their hands saying that nothing can be done from their side and the student can write the next supplementary exam.

Case 2: In the examination hall, a scribe is busy writing the dictation given to her by the visually impaired student. The squad along with the invigilator checks the identity documents of the scribe and rudely reprimands her because she belongs to the higher class and she is not eligible to be the scribe though the girl says that she is a Commerce student writing for an Arts student.

Case 3: Visually challenged student has come to the exam hall with another scribe as the scribe who had written the exam on the previous day was unable to come due to some inconvenience. The authorities take the visually impaired student to task for changing the scribe in the presence of the new scribe. Annoyed scribe doesn't turn up the following day.

Case 4: Scribe is reading out the questions for the visually challenged student who is struggling to recall the answer. There enters a squad and snatches the answer booklet from the scribe saying that the bag of the visually challenged student is kept on the last bench and it has a mobile too. Can a visually challenged student get up and go to the last bench to read the answers from the book? Will there not be an invigilator to monitor all this?

These incidents just give a glimpse of the problems faced by the Visually Challenged students appearing for SSLC, PUC and Undergraduate exams. The woes of these non-sighted students go unheard by the authorities who are in a position to help them. Complicating the situation by showing their supremacy shouldn't be the motto of the sighted people in authority. When we speak of inclusive society, and quote 'Education Is Power' the journey of the visually challenged students in pursuit of Education must be a pleasure and not a pain. The scribes who volunteer to assist the visually challenged students need to be encouraged and supported. The laws and rules need not be taken in a wrong perspective to dissuade the scribes from their noble work. Wrong rules are quoted at times by the concerned authorities due to their ignorance of the law. Hope this letter by Government of India regarding the scribes for the visually impaired during the exams would enlighten the ignorant officials to be more compassionate to handle the **situation with sympathy.**

F.No. 16-110/2003-DD.III

Government of India

Ministry of Social Justice & Empowerment

Department of Disability Affairs

Shastri Bhawan, New Delhi

Dated: 26th February, 2013

To

Principal Secretary/Secretary, Social Welfare of States/UTs.

Subject: Guidelines for conducting written examination for Persons with Disabilities.

Sir,

I am directed to say that Chief Commissioner of Persons with Disabilities (CCPD) in its order dated 23.11.2012 in case No. 3929/2007 (in the matter of Shri Gopal Sisodia, Indian Association of the Blind Vs. State Bank of India & Others) and in case No.65/1041/12-13 (in the matter of Score Foundation Vs. Department of Disability Affairs) had directed this Ministry to circulate guidelines for the purpose of conducting written examination for persons with disabilities for compliance by all concerned. In compliance of the above order, this Ministry hereby lays down the following uniform and comprehensive guidelines for conducting examination for the persons with disabilities as recommended by CCPD:

a. There should be a uniform and comprehensive policy across the country for persons with disabilities for written examination taking into account improvement in technology and new avenues opened to the persons with disabilities providing a level playing field. Policy should also have flexibility to accommodate the specific needs on case-to-case basis.

b. There is no need for fixing separate criteria for regular and competitive examinations.

c. The facility of Scribe/Reader/Lab Assistant should be allowed to any person who has disability of 40% or more if so desired by the person.

d. The candidate should have the discretion of opting for his own scribe/reader/lab assistant or request the Examination Body for the same. The examining body may also identify the scribe/reader/lab assistant to make panels at the District/Division/State level as per the requirements of the examination. In such instances the candidates should be allowed to meet the scribe a day before the examination so that the candidates get a chance to check and verify whether the scribe is suitable or not.

e. Criteria like educational qualification, marks scored, age or other such restrictions for the scribe/reader/lab assistant should not be fixed. Instead, the invigilation system should be strengthened, so that the candidates using scribe/reader/lab assistant do not indulge in mal-practices like copying and cheating during the examination.

f. There should also be flexibility in accommodating any change in scribe/reader/lab assistant in case of emergency. The candidates should also be allowed to take more than one scribe/reader for writing different papers especially for languages.

g. Persons with disabilities should be given the option of choosing the mode for taking the examinations i.e. in Braille or in the computer or in large print or even by recording the answers as the examining bodies can easily make use of technology to convert question paper in large prints, e-text, or Braille and can also convert Braille text in English or regional languages.

h. The candidates should be allowed to check the computer system one day in advance so that the problems, if any in the software/system could be rectified.

i. The procedure of availing the facility of scribe should be simplified and the necessary details should be recorded at the time of filling up of the forms. Thereafter, the examining body should ensure availability of question papers in the format opted by the candidate as well as suitable seating arrangement for giving examination.

j. The disability certificate issued by the competent medical authority at any place should be accepted across the country.

k. The word "extra time or additional time" that is being currently used should be changed to "compensatory time" and the same should not be less than 20 minutes per hour of examination for persons who are making use of scribe/reader/lab assistant. All the candidates with disability not availing the facility of scribe may be allowed additional time of minimum of one hour for examination of 3 hours duration which could further be increased on case to case basis.

l. The candidates should be allowed to use assistive devices like talking calculator (in cases where calculators are allowed for giving exams), tailor frame, Braille slate, abacus, geometry kit, Braille measuring tape and augmentative communication devices like communication chart and electronic devices.

m. Proper seating arrangement (preferably on the ground floor) should be made prior to the commencement of examination to avoid confusion or distraction during the day of the exam. The time of giving the question papers should be marked accurately and timely supply of supplementary papers should be ensured.

n. The examining body should also provide reading material in Braille or E-Text or on computers having suitable screen reading softwares for open book examination. Similarly online examination should be in accessible format i.e. websites, question papers and all other study material should be accessible as per the international standards laid down in this regard.

o. Alternative objective questions in lieu of descriptive questions should be provided for Hearing-Impaired persons, in addition to the existing policy of giving alternative questions in lieu of questions requiring visual inputs, for persons with Visual Impairment.

You are requested to ensure that the above guidelines are scrupulously followed while conducting examination for persons with disabilities. All the recruitment agencies, Academics/Examination Bodies etc. under your administrative control may be advised appropriately to ensure compliance of implementing these guidelines. Action taken in this regard may be intimated to this office.

The above guidelines are issued with the approval of Hon'ble Minister (Social Justice & Empowerment).

Yours faithfully,
(Jagdish Kumar)
Deputy Secretary to the Govt. of India

Copy to: CCPD, Sarojini Bhawan, Bhagwan Dass Road, New Delhi with reference to order dated 23.11.2012 in case No. 3929/2007 and in case No.65/1041/12-13.

This letter is obligatory to all and all need to comply with the conditions mentioned in this. The best solution for the problems faced by the visually challenged students would be when the institutions would take the initiation of motivating their sighted students to volunteer the work of scribe. This assistance of getting a scribe from their teachers would not only be a real blessing for the visually challenged students but also shield them from hunting for a suitable scribe in darkness.

LETTER TO THE MINISTER

From

Prof. Prasanna Udipikar

Bangalore.

Date: February 02, 2017

To

Honorable Minister for Higher Education

Bangalore

Karnataka.

Subject: To set up State Braille Resource Center to encourage more Visually Challenged students to enroll for Higher Education – a request

Esteemed Sir,

At the very outset I would like to congratulate you for working towards the betterment of students and teachers with a vision and mission.

I also take this opportunity to express my gratitude for responding to my letter regarding retaining the Bangalore University Braille Center in the Central College premises to facilitate large number of visually challenged students in and around Bangalore.

I am a professor teaching English to the undergraduate students. My experience of teaching a visually challenged student introduced me to the problems and the trauma the visually challenged students undergo in pursuing higher education.

I was introduced to the problems that the Visually Challenged students undergo during their studies through a visually challenged student of mine – Shilpa S. I appealed to Bangalore University in the year 2011 to provide supportive system to the visually challenged students. As a result **"Committee for the Demographic Study of Visually Challenged Students studying under Bangalore University"** was constituted under the Chairmanship of the Vice Chancellor Dr. Prabhudev in the year 2011 and I was made the Convener. In the academic year 2011-12, the committee introduced the following facilities for the Visually Challenged students studying in Bangalore University:

> ➤ Availability of free text and reference books in Braille font.

> ➤ Availability of free CDs on text books and reference books.

> ➤ Monthly University Scholarship of Rs.500/- for each Visually Challenged Student.

> ➤ Assistance for Scribe availability during exams.

> ➤ Strict monitoring of Green Tape on the Visually Challenged students answer papers for consideration during valuation as per Government orders.

- Supervision during exams on extension of Extra One Hour for the Visually Challenged students.

- Introduction of Special Questions in the University Exam Question Papers exempting pictorial answers for the Visually Challenged students in History, Economics, Statistics and Geography Question Papers.

- Bangalore University Braille Resource Center was set up to conduct Orientation Programmes, Personality Development Programmes, Soft Skills Training, Language Development Programmes, Training in Life Skills, Academic and Personal Counseling, Career Counseling and Placement Activities.

- Maintenance of Statistical data such as number of visually challenged students registered for higher education, number of training courses and the trainees, placement details etc.

Though there were only around hundred and forty five beneficiaries when I started the work, now there are around two hundred visually challenged students who have registered and availing the facilities from the Bangalore University Braille Resource Center.

Sir, you know that all the Universities in Karnataka have not set up Braille Centers. Non-availability of proper guidelines regarding what facilities should be extended and how to reach out to the visually challenged students has hampered the supportive system of the visually challenged students at the university level. None the less, as the Universities are located on the outskirts of the city, accessibility is a problem for the visually impaired students.

Hence setting up of a State Braille Resource Center in Bangalore under the Higher Education Department would be the greatest support any government could do to enable the visually challenged students through education. This State Braille Resource Center would extend various following activities to bring the visually impaired persons to the mainstream of the society:

➢ Providing needed Braille resource material to the Universities to encourage more students to enroll for higher education.

➢ Availability of all the textbooks of respective universities on the website exclusively meant for visually challenged students.

➢ Online coaching for academic progress.

➢ Conducting placement training and other activities.

➢ Distribution of Kindle and other modern supportive systems.

➢ Monitoring and guiding the Universities regarding the new schemes introduced by the government to these students.

> Conducting training programmes for the teachers regarding innovative teaching methodologies to teach visually impaired students.

> Introducing Diploma courses to see that each visually challenged student would complete his/her education with a job in hand or with self employment.

> Maintaining statistics of visually impaired students studying in Karnataka and their placements.

> Availability of all the information connected to visual impairment and the facilities through the website.

Sir, as there is no Center to guide the Universities regarding Enabling the Visually Challenged students, I humbly and earnestly request you to kindly set up a State Braille Center under your leadership which would bring hope, practical relief and a phenomenal change in the lives of Visually Challenged students studying in Karnataka.

With immense faith reposed in your constructive work for the students, I conclude my appeal.

Thank you

Yours faithfully,

Prasanna Udipikar

SAVE THE SIGHT

Refractive error contributes to about 19% of the total blindness worldwide. This is the commonest cause for the life threatening visual impairment. Some of the refractive errors are common among school children and are correctable if identified at the initial stage. In this connection a teacher plays a vital role in identifying the common vision problems among students through some simple classroom activities.

The shape of the eye of a student does not refract or bend light properly; the images appear blurred. Such students find it very difficult to cope with academic activities. In contrast to other normal students, these students with ocular problem may seem very dull, distracted, unfocused, restless, imprecise, confused, non-specific and also at times irritated in the classroom. Kind words, personal attention, consideration and care of the teacher would reveal the shortcomings of the student to the teacher. The teacher can practise some very simple activities in the classroom to identify and save the child from lifetime blindness.

Among Refractive errors some of the most common problems which can be identified by the teacher through classroom games are:

Activity 1: The teacher changes the places of the first row students asking them to occupy last benches and the vice versa. The teacher writes questions and answers on the blackboard and asks each student to write it down in their notebook without copying from their friend's book. As the students are copying down what the teacher has written on the blackboard, the teacher walks between the rows of the benches and observes the posture and writings of the students. The teacher notices that:

> The student who has poor distance vision or **Myopia or Nearsightedness** is unable to read what is written on the blackboard. This student keeps the notes incomplete or tries to copy from friends' books. This can be treated with glasses or contact lenses.

Activity 2: The teacher asks each student to stand up and read the text or answers from the notes. While the students are reading, the teacher observes each student's posture.

> The student who has poor near vision or **Hypermetropia or Farsightedness** finds it difficult to read the text or his own notes. Writing legibly is also difficult for such students. These students hold the book very close to their eyes while reading and writing. This can be treated with glasses or contact lenses.

The other ocular problems which the teacher can observe in a student when the student tries to close his one eye or tilt his head or rubs his eyes frequently etc., for a better vision:

> **Astigmatism** is imperfect curvature of the front surface of the eye, which causes blurred vision or discomfort.

➢ **Anisometropia** is the condition in which both the eyes have different refractive power.

➢ **Amblyopia** is the medical term used when the vision in one of the eyes is reduced because the eye and the brain are not working together properly. The eye looks normal, but it is not being used normally because the brain is favoring the other eye. This condition is also sometimes called lazy eye. Amblyopia is best treated during the preschool years. If untreated, amblyopia can cause irreversible visual loss in the affected eye.

➢ **Strabismus** is a misalignment of the eyes. If the same eye is chronically misaligned, amblyopia may develop in that eye.

These are some of the most common ocular problems found among school-going children. The teacher could sensitize the parents about the problems faced by the child in the classroom academic activities so that the parents would rectify the problem through medical assistance. These activities of the teacher must be done in addition to the Annual Medical Vision Testing Health Programme organised in the schools to save the child from permanent visual impairment. This small step of a teacher would go a long way in keeping the sight aglow.

THE COACH

All the students were pouring into YMCA playground for the Annual Sports Meet. The playground filled with the smiles, laughter and jabbering of the girls. This was a day when the girls could sneak out with their friends and launder on their favourite shopping streets doing window shopping and talking of the latest fashion and the current trend. They were happy that their college did not have a playground and hence every year college authorities hired YMCA playground for the Annual Sports Meet.

The playground was big enough with perfect markings for 100, 200, 400 and 800 meters running race with synthetic track, well maintained high jump courts and shot put, discus throw, javelin throw etc. The college had erected a shamiyana to provide shade for the teachers and guests. The students were permitted to defend themselves against the scorching sun. Colourful caps, sun glasses, umbrellas, Bermuda shorts, track suits of the students highlighted the enthusiasm of the students. Students with sportsman spirit were a few as majority of them came to spend the day in fun and frolic.

YMCA along with renting out its playground also provided PETs (Physical Education Teachers) to organize and judge the events. The Principal had asked YMCA to provide PETs for the payment of Rs.8000/- expecting that they would provide around Four PETs for systematic and smooth run of the events. Hence before the teaching and administrative staff could arrive at the venue, four PETs were already present - three in white sports uniform, white shoes and a cap and one man in yellow shirt with an authoritative voice.

As the events started, the cordless hand speaker was passed on to the man in yellow shirt. He announced the rules for the events and gave final call for the 400 meters and shot put events. The voice was very authoritative and the students obediently followed instructions given.

"Hi……that sir in yellow shirt cajoles students to participate in the events and there are more students enrolling for the events" piqued Sana who had dreamt of grabbing most of the prizes as every year hardly students participated in the events.

"Ya…the sir in yellow shirt is making the competition tougher by enrolling more participants…" Priya added who had also dreamt of getting at least third prize in few events.

The "Sir in yellow shirt" — in yellow shirt middle aged, slightly bald, lean, tall with a long face very soon became quite popular among the girls. None dared to ask his name or get acquainted with him. The Principal and the lecturers were relieved of controlling and coaxing the girls to participate in the events. The "Sir in yellow shirt" seemed to be a very experienced PET with lucid language skills.

"Pump your sprits to Jump high and participate in the High-jump."

"Higher you scale the heights, brighter are your chances of becoming a Champion."

"Students warm up for good takeoff for high-jump."

"Hurry up…Final call for registering your name for High-jump."

One could see the girls hurrying to register their names.

"Wake up to this announcement…stop not till you register your name for the events…enliven up your association with sports through your participation."

"Hurry up…final call for registering your name for High Jump."

One would see the girls hurrying towards the coach in yellow shirt to register their names.

"Wake up to this announcement….stop not till you register your name for the event."

"Associate yourself with the Sport Meet through your sizzling participation."

"Face the challenge, break the barriers, run for relay." His enthusiasm and positive energy was transmitted to the students. More participation of the students gave more work for the man. Any doubts, any clarification, any enquiry by the students were directed to the coach in yellow shirt.

The coaches hired by YMCA wondered why the college had hired them as this coach could manage the entire show alone. They relaxed and assisted the man.

At 5 pm, the Sport Meet came to an end. Everybody hurried to their homes. The tables, chairs, water filter etc brought from the college were loaded into a lorry by the attenders. The coaches of the events surrounded the Principal for their honorarium. An envelope with Rs.8000/- addressed to the authorities of YMCA was handed over with thanks by the Principal to one of the coaches in white uniform. The coach in yellow shirt extended his hand towards Principal for his honorarium. Everybody was taken by surprise.

"Your honorarium is included in that" pointing at the envelope, the Principal smiled.

YMCA coaches said that the man in yellow shirt was not from YMCA.

In fact, the man in yellow shirt belonged to none – neither the college nor YMCA. He was jack of all trades and master of none. He was talented but did not have a job. At cultural activities, he sang and entertained the audience, at wedding he managed the crowd, at road blocks he cleared the traffic... and thus earned his livelihood. He was deprived of school due to poverty, yet had managed to master varied skills.

He had worked hard. He was asking money for his hard labour. But people denied. He begged for some money as they were all satisfied with his honest work. They got annoyed. They threatened him of lodging a complaint against him with the police....the charges would be cheating, trespassing and violating the rules. Power dominates, poverty suffers.

The mighty rule, the weak succumb.

Empty hand, tears filled, with heavy heart the coach in yellow shirt disappeared as the people stood discussing and laughing at him.

CHIMERA

My friend complained that her brother who was 28 years of age had grown to be pessimistic, useless and disgraceful, in short a bundle of lethargic aplomb. I thought of giving a Midas touch to her brother to transform him into being optimistic, useful and graceful in short a bundle of dynamic aplomb. Hoping to see a metamorphic transformation like the caterpillar into a butterfly, I made a debut performance as a psychotherapist in front of this indolent person.

Encasting my most charming smile I tweeted, "How are you?" "Ah! I am fine…strong, happy and healthy as usual. What about you? You look so worried!" He stretched his arms vertically and yawned loudly. I hate to see such a gesticulation as I strongly feel yawning is infectious. Evading his enquiry, I asked, "What are you up now? Any plans of taking up a job or continuing education?" He was quick enough to shoot his answer, "O…no, why should I? Enough of property we have…I am not going to slog and then grumble…I am happy, satisfied and contented with what I am." Wah!…what a rare specimen of contentment! Mustering my spirits I said, "Listen…you are so young and energetic. You shouldn't waste your time sleeping and watching T.V. You must take up a good job and be self dependent."

"And then?"

"Then you would get a beautiful life partner, get married, have your own life."

"And then?"

Not ready to give up my patience I continued, "You can buy the latest model car, possess the best technologies at your disposal, build a model mansion, own a spurious sprawling villa, beget children, grandchildren……."

"And then?"

"You can nicely sleep enjoying your status."

"Ah!…that is what I am doing now…nicely sleeping and enjoying. This is what we would crave to do after achieving so many things in life. Why mess up life? Look how calm and happy I am… Look at yourself…How worked-up, anxious you look!" Oh God! I fumbled for words and then continued, "Human life has a purpose. We need to define life by our actions." "Chimera!…Life according to me is short and sweet." His broad grin unnerved me. He continued, "Think of what happened to Alexander the Great. He realized at the end when he was diseased that his achievements were futile. When you depart from this earth you are not going to take any material possessions or your loved ones along with you. That is why Alexander the Great emperor who died very young due to incurable illness, realized on the death bed that all his wealth and achievements were futile as he could not take them with him after death. Hence he instructed his officials to keep his hands spread out empty when his coffin was being carried. This was to make people realize that one comes to this world empty handed and goes from here empty handed." He continued reflectively, "Desires would lead to sorrow; ambitions could make life disastrous just like the life of Macbeth...So be calm and happy with what you have. And for now bye... bye, I would like to enjoy my siesta." I was aghast at the enormous laid-back attitude of this youngster who was able to tailor the anecdotes and examples of great achievers to suit his negative stance. Leading a worthy meaningful life for him was a chimera – a fantasy, a dream ever unlikely to come true!

MIND – THE SCULPTOR OF MAN

'What is life?' is a question which could be answered with the most powerful adjectives and yet it remains unconvincing and vague. Life of human-beings which is blessed by god with the known manufactured date and unknown expiry date need to be shaped through one's actions. Life can only be given a meaning through one's actions. These actions are the merchandise or facsimile or the reflection of the mind.

Then what does this mind possess? The mind possesses thoughts. Thoughts play a very potent role in shaping one's mind. As John Milton puts it 'Man is what his thoughts are made of.' Angulimala was a 'bad man,' a killer because he had only thoughts with selfish motives of looting and killing for survival. After good thoughts were sowed in his mind by Buddha he became a transformed person. Hence taking care of our thoughts seems to be essential.

Then the question how are the good and bad thoughts generated in one's mind which go into the making of a person? In one of his discourses Sri Sathya Sai gives the formula for this:

Satsanga — Sadvichara — Sadachara.

'Satsanga' refers to good company. People with vision, positive attitude and finer sensibilities need to be around

(Satsanga) by whom a person's thoughts (Sadvichara) would be influenced.

How then these thoughts (Sadvichara) are formulated in the mind? It is by reading or listening to the biographies and autobiographies and inspiring stories. This gives exposure to others lives regarding how to face the trials and tribulations of life.

Good thoughts (Sadvichara) pilot good actions (Sadachara) and thereby go into the making of a person. It is the thoughts which would propel the person to change his life. One of the examples which we must recall here is of Albert Nobel, the scientist who invented dynamite. He did not want people to remember him as an inventor of dynamite but as a man whose name is recalled whenever the highest award Nobel prize is conferred on persons who have excelled in the field of social service, literature or science. Hence it is aptly said 'Think before you act.'

SAKAMMA

Walking in front of the deserted bungalow doomed in darkness on the eve of Mother's Day made me nostalgic. The bungalow held endless reminiscences of Sakamma causing a chill down my spine. The mansion burst with women's laughter, children's dances, men's loud noisy greetings with gin glasses in their hand on Mother's day last year. The whole building was illuminated with colorful incandescent lights and a huge shamiyana with lots of flower pots and perfumed breeze with the whole caboodle to give a celebrations look. The celebration of Mother's Day was on with lots of pomp and show. All the ten children wealthy and well positioned in life with a busy schedule abroad had arrived with their friends and relatives to display their love for their mother - an old lady of 97 years. Sakamma was made to sit on the gilded huge chair with silver colored handles. All the children were busy grinning and smiling at the invitees talking loudly vying with the sugam sangeeth emitted from the imported sound box with woofer which filled the house. I looked at Sakamma who was wrapped in the huge heavy kanjivaram saree...she seemed to be shrunk in embarrassment. Her smile was a mirror to the unbearable hypocrisy of her children. Her eyes couldn't deceive me. I knew what this old mother's heart craved for. It was not for any expensive mobiles, TV, fridge or all the modern gadgets which were found in that bungalow. What she wanted was human companionship to shoo away her reclusiveness.

The Sakamma mansion which stood huge amidst the trees grown by Sakamma in her younger days was the pride of Sakamma, who kept herself busy in taking care of her children. As the children grew, they flew away from Sakamma in search of their passion and building their own dream houses. "Amma, I am a busy businessman and prefer to settle in Dubai" said the eldest. "Amma, I prefer to settle in Sanfrancisco" said the second son. Like this the brood of chickens went away from Sakamma in search of their livelihood. This is natural, but what was unnatural was with these offspring's engrossment in their busy schedule. Old was not gold for them. Money could buy anything in their world. No human companion was with Sakamma as her children felt that Sakamma would be safe alone rather than getting duped by the servants. Sakamma Mansion was children's pride now. Years passed making Sakamma old and fragile, like a leaf turning yellow.

Standing near the gate, Sakamma would wait for people to talk to her. Uninhabited road in the afternoon made her wonder whether the population of the country had drastically come down! In the hot afternoon she waited with jaggery in hand for home returning school children to lure them towards her. The school children sang and danced for the golden ager.

Sakamma's only friends were these school children. The details of their day spent at school was enumerated to

'Ajji' – a word affectionately used by the children to address Sakamma. Sakamma's own children had strictly warned her not to grow intimate with anybody and not to allow anybody inside the house. Sakamma cooked delicious snacks for these children and was gratified on watching them eat it and they appreciated Ajji's culinary art. They kept Sakamma healthy, happy and agile.

But having won the heart of Sakamma who was reluctant to allow anybody into the house as per the order of her children, these school children got an entry into her mansion. Having entered the house, the children were struck by surprise. Inside the huge mansion, all the rooms were locked with a big locks!!! Only one big bedroom, divided into a small kitchen on one side and an attached washroom was Ajji's world!!! Everywhere entry was barred and Sakamma lived like a poor woman in a tiny room!!!

"Ajji, why are all the rooms locked?"

"The locked rooms belong to my children. When they come from abroad they use them."

"What is there in those rooms?" curious Dinnu asked.

"Their valuable belongings."

"Ajji…are you not their precious belonging?"

"Gold, TV, Car, Bunglow, money, property are all precious things to amass. The old life cannot be valued. They don't want to lose me. I am their pride. Hence I am kept safely in this golden cage…They don't want me to strain by cleaning work…one small room with TV, transistor everything I have…they don't want any helpers to be appointed because they dread that I would be harmed… they are my honourable children who are protecting me from evils…they love me so much…"

These school children were her world now. Sakamma had craved for her own children to draw some time out of their busy schedule and talk to her. It was not the physical pain that bothered her; it was the growing terrible loneliness. She had even pretended to be sick to draw their attention but the result was the doctor's visit to her house with a nurse. She felt that she was adding days, months and years to her existence which was of no use for anyone. Scary loneliness gnawed at her. Neither she could reveal it to anyone nor keep it within herself. The great grandchildren whom she had bathed have grown up. Nobody wants her work which she loves to do for them. They don't drink the tea that she prepares as it is of low quality compared to what they usually drink these days. Children told her to watch T.V. and DVDs. They consoled her comparing her to the old poor woman who lives in a hut without any amenities. They called her "lucky" for enjoying all the comforts due to her successful children. The saree that they sent her to wear at home was worth more than Rs.2000/-. They were proud of their way of taking care of their mother. Every year they exhibited their love on Mother's Day lavishly inviting V.I.Ps. The occasion was a get together with hardly anybody to talk lovingly to Sakamma. What the mother of these wealthy children wanted was not the gadgets at home, she wanted human company with whom she could share and talk to her heart's content.

DOVE IN SILKEN THREAD

'I had a dove and the sweet dove died
And I have thought it died of grieving
O! What could it grieve for? Its feet were tied
With a silken thread of my own hand's weaving
Sweet little red feet! Why would you die?
Why would you leave me, Sweet bird, why?'

"But mama…why should the dove grieve? It had all the comforts in the cage…it need not have to go in search of food, its legs were tied with silken thread, it had love of the master, comfort everything…why did it die?" shot my son who was reading John Keats' poem..

Yes, exactly the same questions had engulfed me on hearing the unnatural death of Sania…a doctor one time, born in a middle class family, got married to an affluent business tycoon, a husband who loved her dearly, provided all the comforts, the best things, the best dresses, the best food, the best car and she led an opulent life…but then what was it that pushed her to end her life drastically? The cause of the death of the Dove and this woman of just 29 years was same…lack of FREEDOM. They had everything but they were captives.

Sania had enjoyed four years of her professional life. Being compassionate, she was a much adored doctor… close to the heart of her patients. They believed that it was magical touch that cured them of their ailments and Sania found meaning to life in the eyes of her patients which expressed gratitude.

Marriage came as a manna. The paradigm shift in life was unexpected, unbelievable and unparalleled. Her doting husband put her in trance. Before she could realize what had happened she was a captive. Her husband never allowed her to go to work. He did not want her to practice medicine any more. He sought meaning to everything in terms of money. "When I could buy all beautiful things for my wife, why should she strain herself?" was his argument. He doted on her with rich gifts such as a diamond ring on birthdays, necklace and an outing on the wedding anniversary, visit to malls and films of his choice. There was no reason for her to be sad. He had given her comfortable life, status, affluence…she should and must be happy. He loved to see her playing the role of a typical traditional wife…never argue or express anything against husband's wish! His constraints, love, affection, concern were all suffocation for Sania…so much so that it had strangled her out of life…her life was like the life of the captive dove.

Anand expected his wife to follow the core mantras, that is to be calm, smiling, well dressed, soft spoken, no arguments, accept and respect husband's views and behavior. He wouldn't tolerate any inputs from her whenever he expressed his views on politics or movies. Watching TV programs of her choice in his presence was a question out of place. More talking would also be treated as a characteristic of dominance. Discussing business matters was below his dignity, forget listening to her suggestions or views.

One stern look from her husband would speak volumes about his impatience, anger and intolerance. She shuddered at such behavioral implications. Wife should neatly press his shirts, trousers, kerchiefs, polish shoes sparklingly, meticulously pack tasty lunch, snacks and bid him goodbye with a smile when he left for the office. If wife needed any assistance in her work that was provided. He expected only 'smiles' and 'silences' from his wife.

True…what was it that troubled her? Why was she growing depressed day by day? Wasn't Anand a perfect husband ?..Yeh.. Anand was a perfect husband wanting perfection around. There was no problem…then why did the boredom snare at her? Why was she losing interest in life? She had everything yet what was it that made her at times forget where she was and what she was doing? She shunned the outer world…never felt like sharing her feelings either with her friends or the relatives. She didn't want to be the butt of women talks or gossips, she preferred to project her marital life a bliss.

Sania practiced 'silences' and 'smiles' beyond her capacity…so much that she fumbled for words when her husband spoke to her…she laughed non-stop for a joke cracked by her husband.

The Eight to Eight work schedule of Anand hardly gave any space for him to notice the changes that his wife was undergoing. Draped in beautiful sarees and salwars, Sania looked dazzling and Anand adored his perfect wife! He hardly realized that his extremities were heading towards impending disaster. Wailing over his wife's death, Anand had the same questions as that of the poet to the Dove:

"Sweet little red feet! Why would you die?

Why pretty thing , could you not live with me?

I kissed you oft, and gave you white peas

Why not live sweetly as in the green trees?"

———+)(+———

EDUCATION AND HUMANENESS

"Human beings should develop two unique traits of intellect and humaneness. Technology and Value addition are one of the prime movers of a country's economy."

– Dr. A.P.J. Abdul Kalam.

Education should train students to think and provide solutions to the challenges of the society. Apart from being pillar of strength to human development, formal education should also strongly stimulate the thoughts of an individual's responsibility towards the society. Today students are made to study more from the exam orientation rather than cultivate constructive thinking. Scoring high marks and getting a good job is all that one aims at. Hence education other than helping one to seek a livelihood, should also aim at harnessing the heart giving the students an opportunity to look around and feel. Though text books of High School touch upon the study of great contributors in making the world a better place to live in, there is no methodical structured effort to inform and enlighten the college students regarding what they can do and how they can contribute for eliminating the menaces of the society.

Undergraduate students are mature enough to find and suggest solutions for the problems existing in the country.

As there is no common mandatory platform provided to unravel their hidden potential, it has become a habit with the youngsters to complain about the problems and get used to it. As a result, a sort of hatred and helplessness creeps in the young mind. Tapping the youth power is the dire need of the time for the individual benefit in particular and country's benefit at large. It is high time to educate the heart along with educating the mind.

In this connection, a study on Social Menaces should be made compulsory for the students. This would aim at sensitizing students on various menaces which are lethal to the society. This should be a thought provoking exercise and a platform for the students to contribute for the betterment of the society. An expert committee should be formed to frame the syllabus. The text should enlighten the students about the social menaces at the national level and the state level. Not only the constitutional laws and acts to eradicate the menaces should be taught but also the mention of the contributions of various organizations and individuals towards the removal of the problems should be discussed in the text with interesting examples of the contribution of common man. For example: the hazardous impact of cutting of trees – the role of trees in the maintenance of life on earth – the laws and acts that forbid cutting of trees – the individual contribution namely Salumarada Timmakka in Karnataka and the other environmentalists' contributions towards the issue should be discussed. The syllabus could comprise the topics such as water conservation, garbage management, air pollution, plastic hazards, corruption, pesticides, chemical spray on vegetables and fruits, child marriage, malaria, dengue, stagnant water, pot holes, man holes, careless driving, safety of girl child, implementation of speed governor in the vehicles, overcrowded buses and rickshaws, dowry problem, lives of ragpickers, problems of persons with disability etc.

This study of social menace should be made compulsory for all the streams of college students. 70 marks should be allotted for theory and 30 marks for project work. The project work should comprise case studies, practical reports, documentaries, etc.

A competition at the University Level could be held and the best practical innovative solution provided by the students could be awarded. This would help students to think about the existing problems and provide a solution. The participatory attitude and the urge what best I can give to the society would be kindled among the students. It would be the right age and right time to provide a platform for the undergraduate students to know their country better and contribute their thoughts to the problems. The ideas of young mind would definitely provide a concrete solution to the existing problems.

This would not only bring a phenomenal change in the progressive path of the society but also a tangible contribution towards the holistic development of the students undergoing higher education. A platform provided for the students to think and contribute would unleash their hidden potential making them more responsible citizens with a sensitive heart and mature mind. The ignited minds would produce sparkles of remedies in making the world a better place to live in.

DEALING WITH GARBAGE

I was placed in an obnoxious scene which led to hellish atmosphere in the locality. I couldn't count myself one among those nonchalant people. Mounds of garbage were spread helter-skelter by the dogs, cows, crows and the other 'Rightful Inheritors of the Earth!' The environmental hazard made people pretty stronger…probably increasing the people's immunity! I don't know yet, the secret of people being 'sthitha prajnas.' Neighbours, government agencies, leaders…all remain unfazed. I realized that marching ahead stoically amidst the stinking surroundings was not my cup of tea. I felt I must take a bold and vocal stand. "Waiting for Godot" is fruitless. 'Measure for Measure' is essential. Being obsessed with the idea of clearance or at least reduction of garbage, like an accountant trying to tally the balance sheet, I worked out the varied ways of profitable productivity of garbage. I stood on the other side of a garbage knoll as a sanitary inspector with an intent look at the garbage hillock. Lo.. the dogs ran over the mound and with their rear legs stretched rubbed their body against each other in ecstasy; the cows were busy digging their nose deep into the heap like a gold miner, the innumerable small, fat, lean, black, brown variety of rats with whole set of their brood were nibbling and enjoying hide and seek game, raucous calls of the crows… military disciplined march of the ants, centipedes, hovering flies, insects, mewing cats, grunting pigs…all happily reminding the concept of 'Vasudaivakutumbam!.' But what caught my scrutinizing eyes and provided food for my thoughts was the pile of unsavoured plastics, wrappers and other pieces of dry waste. Yes, I could save Mother Earth from about 40 percent of dry waste percolating into her and also help a ragpicker earn a livelihood and lead a decent life and thereby increase the per capita income of our nation. This would happen only if I could plan for a systematic segregation of waste at its source and disposal of dry waste to the recycling centre.

This thought pushed me forward to act. There was neither any delay nor any hindrance. Technology was put in use to the fullest. I called up my friends in my locality and shared my thoughts. I told them how my mother used to keep aside a fistful of rice in a box every day before she cooked the rice. At the end of every thirty days, the collected rice was cooked and mixed with sambar and was sent for the inmates of the leprosy ashram. This was done by many people and the inmates everyday had sumptuous meals. 'Narayana Seva' was the name given to this activity.

I applied this theory to the 'donation' of dry waste. I motivated my friends to keep aside every day in the kitchen in a gunny bag, dry waste that they came across at home which includes empty toothpaste tubes, milk sachets, shampoo sachets, plastic covers, chocolate-biscuit wrappers, empty bottles, used plastic water bottles, empty packs, empty ice-cream cups, tetra packs, tins, foil wrappers, used paper glasses, paper plates, paper napkins, broken dolls, torn bags, old clothes.. each and every dry waste and hand them over once a week to a ragpicker who would further segregate and sell the same to the recycling centers.

We could help him to eke out a living by our 'daana' or 'donation.' My words clicked. The word 'daana' of trash was appealing. No money is involved in this virtuous work! Now nearly fifty houses in my locality donate the trash which is accepted as a treasure by the ragpicker who comes once every week…now in a mini-van. Tonnes of dry waste are being saved from polluting the environment. Sure this can be done in every locality? Reader…would you also try this 'daana?'

BEWARE!...CHAMELEONS AROUND!

Life in its varied hues has chameleons to increase its perplexity and severity. At times the chameleonic quality becomes the nature of persons in yielding their livelihood. These human chameleons could be in any garb starting from a politician to a beggar on the roadside. Unaware of the chameleonic schemes, the commons fall prey to their deceptiveness. Their luring of the victim is so schematic that the victim hardly realizes the spell of the chameleons.

"Akka...give me alms."

— Silence —

"Akka, God has blessed you to give and Yellamma devi has blessed me to receive from you...don't turn your face and be the cause for God's wrath" the gruff voice grunted.

I, who dread human wrath, couldn't even imagine being prey to the Almighty's wrath! Ha...never.

Without any dillydallying I dropped a coin of Rs.5/- into her extended hand by slightly lowering the window glass. So doing I looked into her eyes intently.

Sitting alone in the car parked on the deserted lane, the sight of this woman was scary.

Jet black big face with pan smeared lips, reddish teeth, drowsy eyes, vermillion-turmeric plastered forehead, manly built physic, is it a woman with a shaved face…or a man in woman's dress…???

A fiend!!! No…it was 12 noon. How can ever a female evil spirit dare to manifest during day time?

The sorceress smiled…a weird, vicious smile…which sent a shudder down my spine.

"Akka, don't you want to know your future…I follow God's verdict…I have been sent to foretell your future… you are very innocent with a kind heart rarely found in this Kaliyuga…your face is so graceful, your eyes express your passion to be good and to do good, you have immense faith in God and the vice-versa..You are Laxmi…"

I smiled getting carried away by her mellifluous words……though a stranger how rightly s/he has understood me…I blushed!!!

"You are truthful, honest and straight forward…you are as soft as butter and easily melt at people's suffering… you are…"

Lo…I observed that the woman/man was trying to push down the window glass and meddling with the car door. Luckily I had closed all the windows and only one window on my right was slightly open through which s/he tried to pass prasadam to me…I prayed fervently to God to be my Saviour…

Hey Bhagawan…daya karo…krupa karo…Raksha karo…bhagawan…

Is this woman/man trying to loot me or snatch my gold accessories by such gimmicks?

The GOD within me woke up and cautioned me not to be unnerved, but to be bold and courageous.. . I must show her that I am not Laxmi but Durga or Kali…Bhadra Kali..

I told her in a stern voice to go or else I would call the police. I took my mobile to dial 100.

Before I could dial for help…a miracle occurred…a man in police dress came near the fiend and took her by hand. An auto came to ferry them and the policeman pushed her into it and they hurriedly disappeared. When I was still in trance, my people were in front of me making me realize the cause for the hurried desertion of those rogues!!!

I thanked my stars for saving me from being victimized by these chameleons.

INCORRIGIBLE MOSQUITOES

I put on record and declare vociferously that I hate mosquitoes. I can tolerate cockroaches in the kitchen closets, lizards on the walls, earthworms in the bathrooms, ants on the kitchen slab, houseflies and centipedes during monsoons etc., but not mosquitoes. These harmless creatures at the most would elicit an alarm from me or a jump or a shudder. But mosquitoes though they do not evoke any of such reactions, I despise them from the bottom of my heart. Gleefully I read out aloud from a paper that mosquitoes are in no way useful on earth except for being irritant, deadly, poisonous, miasmic, fatal, mephitic, virulent, noxious......string of negative adjectives I could use to empty the cauldron of my distaste for mosquitoes.

I cannot forget my experience which caused cancellation of my much awaited tour to Varanasi.

That fat black big mosquito sat on my ankle and within no time grew fatter; my impulse forced me to murder it ruthlessly....the blood spattered "Yet who would have thought the old man to have so much blood in him?" I contemplated with the words of Lady Macbeth replacing the 'old man' with the 'old mosquito.'

Consequential action was rubbing my hand rigorously with water to clean the splashed blood of the mosquito on my palm. Like for Lady Macbeth, the sight of the blood on my palm was obnoxious. I recalled the dialogue of Lady Macbeth in her sleep walking scene:

"Yet, here's a spot…out, damned spot! Out. Here's the smell of the blood still: all the Perfumes of Arabia will not sweeten this little Hand…(what's done cannot be undone!)"

Unlike Lady Macbeth, my obsession was more to do with the sight of the blood rather than the smell of the blood. I cleansed my soul of the cruelty meted out to the mosquito by rendering half an hour extra prayer.

That night was unusual. Rain slashed heavily outside complimented by thunder and lightning. The murdered mosquito might have been a community leader or a revolutionist. A swarm of mosquitoes invaded the room to attend the funeral…mourning loudly and cursing my body. No mosquito repellents worked that night and I was left in darkness guilt stricken shrouded in mystery.

Afflicted by my crime, I lose my confidence and see that my body temperature had increased. Excruciating pain took over my joints and it was miserable even to change sides. Pain spread in circular motion like the ripples of water caused due to a stone throw on the calm surface of the river. Moments of peace had lost. Prospero's curse to Caliban in Shakespeare's play *The Tempest* echoed in my ears "For this, be sure, to-night thou shalt have cramps, side-stitches that shall pen thy breath up; urchins shall, for that vast of night that they may work, all exercise on thee; thou shalt be pinched as thick as honeycomb, each stinging than bees that made them."

O…oh…o…oh…o…oh the dawn saw me battered and shattered, dishevelled hair, dark circles around the sleepless deep set eyes, parched tongue, reddish long drawn face, weary feverish pulsating body of mine was wheeled to the doctor who declared that I had Poly Arthritis fever with terrible joints pain infected by a virus injected into my body by a 'MOSQUITO.' Certainly the vengeful mosquito had won in its mission – posthumously!!!

Share your views at: prasannaudipikar@gmail.com